FOLKLORE AND
IN DO
AND WIL

Written by John C. Chadwick
Illustrated by Kate Mayely/Lindsey Greenhill
ISBN No. 0 907683 12 6

"I would like to thank the staff of Wilton Public Library for their help."

N. J. Clarke Publications
Tollgate Cottage
Tappers Knapp
Uplyme
Lyme Regis
Dorset
Telephone: Lyme Regis (02974) 3669

CONTENTS

Page

LOCAL CUSTOMS
The Byzant Ceremony — The Dorset Ooser 2
The Skimmity Ride — Going A'Shroving 4
Oak Apple Day — Out for a Duck 5
Midsummer Day 6
Hallowe'en 7
The Giant and Hob-nob 8

GHOSTS
The Spectral Ape and Others 9
The Drowning Smuggler 10
The Monk and the Martyr — An Unusual Hotel 11
The Phantom Coach — Wild Darrell 12
The Demon Drummer 13
The Bishop's Birds 14

SUPERSTITIONS
Creatures Great and Small 16
Birds 17
Trees and Plants 18
Weather 19
At Home 21

WITCHCRAFT
Witches Corner 23
The Stalbridge Witches — Jinny Gould Gate 24
The Witch of Spettisbury —
Two Modern Witches — Lyddie Shears 25
The Odstock Curse 26
The Potterne Witch 28

TRADITIONAL CURES AND HERBS 29
WHAT'S IN A NAME? 32
SOME DORSET SAYINGS 33
WILTSHIRE'S CURIOUS CHARACTERS
The Flying Monk 34
Rattlebone — Bonham's Babies 35
Maud Heath — Ruth Pierce 36
The Wiltshire Moonrakers 37

FOREWORD

Adder's fork, and blind-worm's sting,
Lizard's leg, and howlet's wing,
For a charm of powerful trouble,

Like a hell-broth boil and bubble.

Macbeth

What part of Britain is richer in folk-history than Wessex? This great treasure chest overflows with fascinating tales of witchcraft, superstition, ghosts and traditions from the building of Stonehenge down to Thomas Hardy's day. Here is a selection of just a few of the high-lights from the East Dorset and Wiltshire regions of Wessex.

LOCAL CUSTOMS

The Byzant Ceremony

Shaftesbury stands 700 feet above the Blackmore Vale. In Tudor times, the hill-dwellers had a water problem which was solved by bringing up supplies from Enmore Green in the Manor of Gillingham below.

Every year, in return for this right, after an hour's dancing to minstrels' music, the Mayor of Shaftesbury presented the Lord of the Manor with a pair of white gloves, a loaf of bread, a calf's head and a gallon of ale. He was also offered the Byzant, a kind of besom or corn dolly, decked with ribbons, feathers and jewels said to be worth £2000. This was handed back and the rest of the day spent in feastoing and revelry.

The Byzant Ceremony is still periodically re-enacted in June, with the chief characters and their attendants dressed in colourful Tudor costume. In its present form, the Byzant looks like a large, over-decorated, gold table lamp. Its name might come from 'bizant' (Anglo-Norman) for 'offering') or from 'besom' (a cleansing agent like water).

The Dorset Ooser

'Watch out or the Ooser'll get 'ee,' was how Dorset parents in by-gone days would threaten their wayward children. Every village, then, had it's Ooser (perhaps derived from the old word 'guiser' or mummer). This was a mask worn on special occasions such as May Day or Christmas, when the wearer would prance and bellow to scare the wits out of his audience.

The mask had a lower jaw moved by string to gnash the teeth. It had crisp hair, whiskers, beard and a formidable pair of horns. The forehead showed a big bump and the eyes started out in hatred, terror and despair.

THE OOSER MASK

The original Ooser was an ancient, pagan, bull-like god. In pre-Christian times, tribal priests wore his mask at fertility rites.

Shillingstone was one of his longest surviving strongholds and the Melbury Osmond mask — the last known traditional one — disappeared around 1900. Fortunately a photograph turned up from which a new mask was fashioned at Weymouth in 1973 to inspire the gyrations of a morris-dancing organisation. So Dorset has its Ooser again.

The Skimmity Ride

Another occasion for the Ooser's appearance was the Skimmington or Skimmity Ride. This brutal custom once flourished throughout Dorset. It was a public demonstration against misbehaviour, usually of the mixed-up marriage sort like adultery — a kind of matrimoniall lynch-law.

About dusk, a procession would form up and parade the culprits' effigies on donkey-back through the streets, to the sound of beaten kettles and trays. Stops were made at the culprits' homes and every inn on the way. Finally the effigies were hung and burnt.

The most dramatic description occurs in Thomas Hardy's 'The Mayor of Casterbridge' (Dorchester). The rabble protest savagely against the indiscretions of Henchard and Lucetta by arranging the customary barbaric procession. The lovers get the lot — effigy, donkey, hostile mob and band of ram's-horns, tambourines, cleavers, tongs, serpents and humstrums.

The name Skimmington probably comes from the skimming-ladle used in the procession.

Going A'Shroving

Pancakes have come on Shrove Tuesday from time imemorial. Perhaps they were made to use up the housewife's eggs and fat before the Lenten fast.

An old account from Milton Abbey of some other strange customs — now defunct — could have applied to many other parishes. Children would go 'Lent-crocking' from house to house, singing some version of this rhyme:

> 'I be come a'shroving
> For a little pancake,
> A bit o' bread o' your baking,

Or a little truckle cheese o' your making
If you'll gi' me a little I'll axe thee no more,
If you don't gi' me nothing I'll rattle your door.'

As a result they were given halfpennies, apples, pancakes, or cheese. If they got nothing, broken crockery and other missiles were hurled at the door.

Even more unpleasant pastimes included badger-baiting, cock-fighting and cock-squailing, when stones were thrown at a tethered cock.

Oak Apple Day

Great Wishford lies peacefully beside the Wiltshire river Wylye. Above it stretches Grovely Wood, a dark, mysterious, prehistoric forest, belonging to the Earl of Pembroke. On Oak Apple Day (29th May), the villagers still celebrate their victory, a couple of centuries ago, over the Earl, who had tried unsuccessfully to overrule their ancient rights to gather the forest's green branches.

Before dawn, a tin-pan band rouses the villagers from their beds and sends them on their way to cut the forest's oak boughs. These are brought down to decorate their houses and the top of the church tower.

A mid-morning bus then takes a delegation the eight miles to Salibury Cathedral: here they affirm their rights by offering green boughs to the Dean at the altar and giving the traditional cry: 'Grovely! Grovely! Grovely! and all Grovely!' After a dance in period costume in the Close, they return to Wishford for a formal lunch, followed by a fete.

Out for a Duck

The thresher-poet Stephen duck is unknown today but every year on 1st June, a Duck Feast is held by farmers in his memory at the Charlton Cat Inn on

Salisbury Plain.

Born at Charlton in 1705, he was a farm labourer before his poetic talent came to the notice of Queen Caroline and her Court. But the novelty soon wore off and he was ignored. After taking Holy Orders, he later committed suicide.

Lord Palmerston admired his poems and provided funds for the annual Feast at the inn. Here his relics are still preserved — a book of his poems, the ⅝-pint Duck Glass and the Duck Hat, decorated with feathers and a thresher's pictuere.

At the Feast, the Chief Duck Man wears the Hat. He and the eleven other members must each repeat, without faltering, the traditional toast: 'In memory of Lord Palmerston and the Rev: Stephen Duck', and drain the Glass without taking his lips from the rim. Anyone making a mistake must drink the toast again at his own expense or a fine.

Midsummer Day

The only thing certain about Stonehenge, Britain's greatest prehistoric monument, is that it is there. Astronomers and archaeologists still argue about its origin and purpose. The 17th century antiquary John Aubrey was one of the first to associate Stonehenge with the Druids, who still come here to worship the sun.

On Midsummer Day, after a midnight vigil, they arrive in procession as the light gets stronger. Dressed in white robes, they carry banners and other emblems. The rites then begin, followed by the forming of a ring in the middle of the stone circle.

The Druids now wait for the sun to align itself just above the Heel Stone, which stands a short way outside the circle to the northeast. When the great moment comes, they acknowledge the dawn by blowing long, bronze horns.

Recently the ceremony has degenerated into a sort of free festival for vast crowds of Wallies, wierdos, drug-pushers and even worse.

Hallowe'en

On Hallowe'en (31st October) — the Witches' Sabbath — the covens would gather to perform their rites in the circle carved by the high priestess with her ceremonial black knife.

It was thought unwise to sleep on Hallowe'en, so people took the opportunity to find out about the future from the many spirits in circulation that night.

For instance, you peeled an apple in one piece and threw the peel over your left shoulder. On the floor it would reveal the initial of the person you were to marry. Or a girl, not afraid to sleep, would expect to glimpse her future husband in a dream, if she put a sprig of rosemary and a crooked sixpence under her pillow.

If you spent the night in the churchyard, at midnight a procession of those who were to die during the coming year would enter the church.

Apple-bobbing is still popular at Hallowe'en and many of the other old customs have been adapted as party games.

The Giant and Hob-nob

Today the Giant and Hob-nob live in the Salisbury Museum. They still appear in procession through the streets on special occasions, such as coronations, jubilees, pageants and carnivals.

The Giant is about twelve feet high and has a dusky face with large staring eyes and bushy, black beard. He wears medieval costume which conceals his bearer,. Hob-nob is a fine specimen of the hobby-horse which featured in old-time plays.

The origins of the Giant are uncertain but he was called Saint Christopher in the Middle Ages, when the Tailors' Guild took him over. The Guild provided the clothing for his attendant esquires, morris-dancers, black boys and devil.

The Giant and Hob-nob's frequent parades through Salisbury during the last century were often both ribald and rowdy. The two would chase round after the girls, to the music of flute and drum, while the ale flowed freely to stimulate the dancers.

The Family Crest of the Martin Family, features the spectered Ape

GHOSTS

The Spectral Ape and Others

High up in the Hauntings League is Athelhampton Hall, a beautiful 15th century house on the outskirts of Puddletown. It has at least six ghosts. All have been seen or heard recently, except one.

The exception is the Spectral Ape, in life a pet monkey of the Martyn family, who once lived here. Its pathetic ghost haunts a secret staircase. The story goes that a Martyn girl, disappointed in love, went up the staircase to the room above and committed suicide. In her distress she slammed the door at the top of the stairs, not realising that the tame monkey had been following her. The poor thing was trapped on the staircase and died of starvation.

Not long ago, two people saw the Grey Lady. The first was a housemaid, who saw her sitting in the Tudor Room just after the departure of the last of the day's visitors. The maid politely asked her to go, as the house was now closed to the public. The Grey Lady promptly left — through the wainscot.

The housekeeprer also saw her sitting in the same room, wearing 'a rather full, plain dress and a gauzy sort of head-dress....then she gradually faded away'.

Another maid saw the Black Priest. Thinking she heard footsteps, she turned to find him standing there, plainly visible, outside a bathroom door. It was broad daylight and he looked like a hooded monk. This ghost was probably once a priest of the Martyn family, who were Catholics.

A curious tale is told about the Ghostly Duellists. A lady guest was sitting in the Great Hall between tea and dinner. Suddenly two young men entered the room. They ignored her and started to duel. Very upset, she requested them to stop but they took no notice. When she rang the bell to summon a servant there was no response. Meanwhile the men continued their duel until one of them was wounded in the arm, whereupon they left the room. Later the lady's host could offer no explanation.

Finally, the Phantom Cooper has been heard hammering on barrels long removed from a cellar next to the Great Hall.

The Drowning Smuggler

Spine-chilling cries have been heard as the moon

wanes over Worbarrow Bay, near Lulworth. About three centuries ago, a smuggler was caught there by revenue men, who stoned him to death. Enclosed by the rising tide, he threshed around in the water and screamed in agony as he desperately struggled to avoid the stones.

The Monk and the Martyr

Little remains today of the once splendid Abbey of Shaftesbury. It was demolished when Henry VIII ordered the Dissolution of the Monasteries in 1539. Before the end, the last Abbess Elizabeth Zouche instructed one of the monks to bury the great treasure of the Convent of Saint Edward.

This he did but dropped dead before he could reveal its whereabouts. His ghost is said to walk the Abbey grounds, vainly trying to tell someone where to find it among the ruins.

Gold Hill — steep, cobbled and much photographed — leads up to the Abbey. Here the ghosts of two men with pack-horses have been seen. They are bringing for burial the body of young King Edward the Martyr from Corfe Castle, where in 978 he was murdered, probably on his stepmother's orders. His relics and grave can be seen by visitors to the Abbey today.

An Unusual Hotel

The strange happenings — which have recently eased off — within the Crown Hotel in Poole have been recorded often enough. But no explanation of the cause seems to have been provided.

The manifestation takes the form of a small, white ball of fluorescent mist, which travels from the back through to the main entrance.

The sounds of a piano being played come from a

room upstairs: then follows the thud of a falling body and the noise of it being dragged across the floor. Even when bolted, the door of this room opens on its own, whereupon the white ball appears.

The Phantom Coach

At Wool, among the reeds by the old bridge, stands Woolbridge Manor. This desolate, tall-chimneyed, Elizabethan house once belonged to the Turbervilles, a very old Dorset family, whose headquarters were at Bere Regis, five miles away.

It is said that a phantom coach-and-four runs between the two houses. However it appears only to those with Turberville blood in their veins: disaster is supposed to come to any member of the family who sees it.

In Thomas Hardy's 'Tess of the D'Urbervilles', the heroine and Angel Clare set out for their ill-fated honeymoon at 'Wellbridge' in an old-fashioned post-chaise. Tess remarks that she seems to have seen it before. In reply Angel reminds her of the legend of the D'Urberville of bygone days committed a terrible crime. Hardy never falsified the legends of his beloved Wessex.

Wild Darrell

Dorset's Athelhampton Hall is rivalled in number of ghosts by the seven of Littlecote, near Marlborough. Three of them are linked in a story which began one stormy night in 1575. A local midwife was taken blindfold to a large house where a masked lady was in labour. When the child was born, a man 'of haughty and ferocious looks' snatched the baby and stamped it into the fire with his boot.

The midwife managed tp snip a piece from the bedhangings. This evidence brought Wild William

Darrell of Littlecote to trial, but he was acquitted. Curiously enough, the Judge — Sir John Popham — inherited the house on Darrell's death.

This occured a few months after the trial, when he was thrown from his horse and broke his neck. It is said that his horse shied at the apparition of the murdered child. The spot became known as Darrell's Style. It is haunted by his ghost and his phantom hounds, at which horses still shy.

The murder room is haunted by a distracted woman holding a baby. But who was the masked lady? It might have been the wife of Sir Henry Knyvett or Darrell's mistress Elizabeth Bonham or even his own sister Rachel. Nobody knows but there is no doubt about the identity of the father.

Other Littlecote ghosts include three women, one seen in the Chinese bedroom, one carrying a rushlight and one, perhaps a Popham, in the garden. A tenant after the first World War named Gerard Lee Bevin, later convicted of embezzlement, is said to haunt the Long Gallery.

The Demon Drummer

Tidworth was the scene of the disturbance caused by the Demon Drummer. The story goes that in 1661 a wandering drummer was jailed in Gloucester. His drum was confiscated and taken to the Magistrate's house in Tidworth. Nasty things then began to happen there.

To the rataplan of a ghostly drum, clothes were wrenched from beds and children's hair was torn by invisible hands. There were mysterious knockings and objects moved about of their own accord.

This continued for months, until the investigations of a Royal Commission resulted in the drummer admitting his guilt. He was sentenced to transportation, but he — or his ghost — managed to come back and continue the drumming.

The Bishop's Birds

The Bishop's Birds are said to appear when a Bishop of Salisbury is dying. They are as large as albatrosses and of dazzling whiteness, with very long wings which do not seem to beat the air.

In 1885 Miss Moberly saw two of them rise from the grounds of the Bishop's Palace and fly away westwards. A couple of hours earlier the Bishop, her father, had died.

One evening in 1911 Edith Oliver, the writer, was

returning home to Wilton by horse-brake from a choir-boys' outing to Wardour. At Hurdcott she saw two huge white birds sailing over the meadows. Back home she learnt that the Bishop had died unexpectedly.

The Birds Signal The Bishop's Death!

SUPERSTITIONS

Creatures Great and Small

In Dorset the best way of keeping witches and fairies from your house was to put in the chimney a bullock's heart stuck full of thorns, nails or pins. If your cat was to be a good mouser, it had to be given not bought. When a shrew-mouse ran over a man's foot he would go lame. Should an adder bite you, its fat could heal the wound.

Bees swarming in the roof of a house foretold the householder's death. A young bumble-bee coming indoors meant that a stranger would arrive that day. To drive it out brought ill luck.

If you swung a money-spider three times round your head by it's thread and then pocketed it, money would soon come your way. Whenever you saw a toad, you had to spit or throw a stone at it, to keep off it's evil effects.

Old Wiltshire villagers were convinced that hedgehogs sucked milk from cows lying in meadows. They also swore that hedgehogs visited orchards and carried the apples away on their spines.

On Christmas Eve tradition had it that cattle turned to the east and knelt to adore the Child in the Bethlehem manger. It was believed too that at this season cattle received the gift of speech but that it was dangerous to listen to them.

Foxes were seen to rid themselves of their fleas by holding a tuft of sheep's wool in their mouth. Then they went into water, leaving only nose-tip and wool above the surface. The fleas took refuge on the wool, which the fox promptly ditched.

Wiltshire shepherds thought it unluckey to count their lambs before lambing finished. It was also unlucky if the first lamb dropped was black — black twins brought worse luck. With white twins came good fortune to the whole flock.

Carters would string up hag stones (which had a natural hole through them) in the stable to protect horses from disease and prevent them from being ridden by witches.

Birds

'There, I could tell I was going to hear of something, 'cause our cocks crowed so in the night,' an old Dorset villager remarked on hearing of the death of a relative. A cock crowing at the door meant a visitor was coming.

Before putting a broody hen on the eggs, it was the custom to tuck it's head under the right wing and swing the bird round till it fell asleep. It was unlucky to set a hen on an even number of eggs.

Children were warned that if they ever stole an egg from a robin's nest, their little fingers would grow crooked. To kill a robin was sure to bring disaster.

Wood-pigeons' feathers always had to be got rid of and never used to stuff beds or pillows: it was thought that a person could not die peacefully when lying on them. Peacocks' feathers kept in the house brought bad luck.

As a Wiltshire parson lay dying, the neighbouring owls gathered in large numbers to perch all over his rectory. When he died they flew away. But as his coffin was being carried through the lychgate to the church, a big, white barn owl swooped right down on it, before vanishing into a near-by yew tree.

If they met a single jackdaw or crow, many Wiltshiremen would raise their hat and say 'Good morning, Jack.' This salutation averted evil. Should a magpie perch on a roof, it signified that the roof was sound: no tree used by a magpie would ever be uprooted.

On hearing the cuckoo for the first time, you were wise to turn your silver and make a wish. If you were standing on soft ground, an easy time lay ahead but hard ground meant hard times.

When swallows built under the eaves, the birds were said to protect the house from thunder and lightening. Desertion of a nest foretold bad luck but to destroy it brought dire calamity.

Trees and Plants

Dorset girls used to test their lovers' faithfulness by putting an apple pip in the fire. If it burst, all was well but if it burned in silence, he was false. A good apple crop was expected if the sun was seen shining through the branches of an apple tree on Old Christmas Day (6th January).

Farmers used to place a prematurely born calf in the fork of a maiden ash, head pointing east. This prevented other cows in his herd from casting their calves.

To find her future husband, a girl would walk through the garden at Midsummer with a rake over her left shoulder. Throwing hemp-seed over the other, she chanted:

> 'Hemp-seed I set, hemp-seed I sow,
> The man that is my true-love
> Come after me and mow.'

Her future husband should then appear behind her with a scythe.

On bringing the season's first daffodils indoors, there must be a lot of them or your poultry would fail.

To smell white roses was bad for your health, but smelling red ones was good for it.

Old time Wiltshire countrymen always chopped willow. They thought it unlucky to use a saw and carry the logs inside for burning. But hawthorn brought good luck and village maypoles were usually made of it. A sprig in the cowshed ensured good milking.

Newly-wed couples moving into a cottage often planted periwinkles in the garden to bring them a happy marriage,. The white bryony is the English equivalent of the mandrake. The big root is not unlike a crude human figure. When dug up, a demon inside it was supposed to utter such a terrible shriek that anyone hearing it would drop dead.

Burning elder wood was thought to bring the Devil into the house. Lay a child in a cradle made of elder and it would pine away or be cruelly nipped by the fairies. Whipping with an elder stick stunted a child's growth. Ivy growing on a house kept those inside from harm, but a sudden withering would bring misfortune.

Weather

Here are a couple of Dorset long-range weather forecasts:

> "Sun Easter Day,
> Little grass, but good hay,
> Rain Easter Day,
> Good deal of grass, but bad hay."

A warning about early frosts went:

> "A frost before Michaelmas Day
> Hard enough to bear a duck,
> All the winter after
> Nothing but muck."

The old saying that "A green Christmas makes a full churchyard" suggested that a hard spring might prove fatal to the sick and elderly who had survived a mild winter.

When the moon was "lying on her back" (with the tips pointing right up) a wet month was predicted. Should the new moon appear on a Saturday, sailors had a particular dread of the weather to come.

A curious Dorset belief of the last century was that the music of the itinerant German bands brought bad weather. If a countryman saw cattle feeding at the top of a hill during wet weather, he could expect that it would soon clear up. When geese flew or fluttered uphill, good weather was on the way.

The writer Ralph Whitlock has told how the young people of Wiltshire soon learnt the signs of coming rain. Moles threw up larger hills; geese got together and honked; toads became active; sheep rose early to graze; elderly cats behaved like kittens and most cats washed behind their ears; spiders waited at the entrance to their webs; green woodpeckers called; rooks fed in the fields near their rookeries. Pigs could see the wind and knew when it would bring rain.

The first twelve days of January were thought to foretell what the weather would be like in the coming year. According to an old saying:

"As many mists in March you see,
So many frosts in May will be."

Another belief was that killing a black slug would always ensure rain within twenty-four hours. But nobody ever dared do this, even in the severest drought, because of the terrible luck it would also bring.

At Home

When a spark from a log fire flew out at you, according to an old Dorset saying, you should immediately spit at the fire. This saved you from losing your temper with someone later.

If, by mistake, you put on an article of clothing inside out, you were likely to get a present. To change it back would cancel your good fortune. Your hair was never to be carelessly thrown away, because if it was used for lining a magpie's nest, you would be dead within a year.

It was thought unlucky for people to pass each other on the stairs. Tripping on the way down was also unlucky but stumbling upstairs was a good omen.

In Wiltshire a guest room was not to be swept until its recent occupant had left the house by at least an hour. Otherwise the guest might have an unpleasant journey.

If two women poured tea from the same brew, one of them would give birth that year. Sharpening a knife after sunset signified that a thief or an enemy would break in.

Two friends washing their hands in the same water would quarrel unless they spat in the basin. A new garment would wear badly if washed for the first time under the new moon.

It was said that your bed should always be positioned east/west — never north/south — otherwise you would have nightmares. It was unlucky to get out of bed on the opposite side to the one you got in.

Burning ears meant someone was talking about you. If your left hand itched, you would get money, but an itching right hand predicted paying it out.

A baby had to be carried upstairs before being taken down, to ensure that it would "rise in life." The saying "Soon teeth — soon toes" indicated that if a baby's teeth appeared quickly, there would soon be an addition to the family.

WITCHCRAFT

Witches Corner

A desolate part of Leigh Common, near Wimborne, was the reputed meeting place of witches. Here, centuries ago, spells were cast by night on intended victims. A waxen image of the victim was made, christened and pricked with pins. After dancing and chanting, the witches held the image to a fire and as it melted, the victim was willed to "pine away." 17th century magistrates had to take action. Thereafter the scene of these revels, handy to a ducking pond, was known as Witches' Corner.

The Stalbridge Witches

Stalbridge was another thriving witches' nest. Their queen, Mother Hurn, was acclaimed by rich and poor for her predictions and her cures for sick people and animals. Though her home was a reeking shambles, she was a "white" or benevolent witch, using her powers to offset the "black" art of her local rivals.

Stalbridge had male witches too. One old man cured warts. Asked how it was done, he said: "I d'blow 'em to the moon." A girl with toothache consulted another old man. As they talked, the pain disappeared. Then he twisted a piece of paper into a true lover's knot and said: "Sew this into your stays and never undo it or you'll git toothache again." This she did and remained free from pain for years. Then one day, out of curiosity, she removed the paper, read some mysterious letters on it and threw it away. Immediately the toothache returned.

Jinny Gould Gate

The old witch Jinny Gould lived near an ancient Toll Gate at Ulwell, between Studland and Swanage. One night a home-going carrier, full of ale, saw a dirty great cat sitting on the top of the gate. Something about the cat needled him and he whipped it savagely across the back. Whereupon it vanished into thin air.

Next day they found Jinny dead in her cottage, with a cruelly lacerated back. In later years, "Jinny Ghoul Gate" was reputed to open automatically for late-night travellers.

The Witch of Spettisbury

A witch who once lived near Spettisbury enjoyed weird powers of persuasion. She could immobilise animals by just staring hard at them. Cattle being driven past her door to market could be stopped and horses on their way to the fields held up. So the local farmers were careful to keep on the right side of her and those uncanny powers brought in a steady income.

Two Modern Witches

Witchcraft is still very much alive. A Dorchester lady claimed to have used her gifts in the summer of 1969 for a political purpose. Calling up the aid of Mr. John Strachey, the War Minister, as her spirit guide, she cast a spell on Brigadier Woods, the Commandant of Bovington Camp. He was killed when his helicopter crashed.

Not long ago, a Wimborne woman boasted that she had got rid of an unpleasant husband by bewitching him. Within three weeks, to the astonishment of his friends, he dropped down dead.

Lyddie Shears

The notorious Winterslow witch, Lyddie Shears, flourished in the first half of the last century. She used to flog gypsy goods to cottagers and only those brave enough to refuse her were able to keep out of her clutches. Poachers would ply her with tobacco and snuff to get her to go out and attract hares for them to knock down.

The story goes that she often turned herself into a hare which a farmer named Tanner used to course with his greyhounds. But the hare always vanished on reaching her garden, much to the annoyance of the farmer. So he consulted the rector of Tytherley, who suggested that he made a bullet from a sixpenny-piece.

The farmer took this advice and with the bullet shot the evasive as it went into the garden. Later they found the body of Lyddie Shears lying dead on the floor of her cottage with a silver bullet in her heart. This was the traditional way of killing a witch.

The Odstock Curse

The story of the Odstock Curse is high drama. It begins in 1801, when a gypsy was hanged in Salisbury. His name was Joshua Scamp and he came from the near-by village of Odstock.

He had been found guilty of stealing a horse on the evidence of his coat being discovered in the stable from which the horse had disappeared. The coat had been purposely left there by his son-in-law, who was the real culprit. However, to protect his daughter, who was expecting a baby, he refused to plead. Only after his death came the acknowledgment of his innocence.

He was buried in Odstock churchyard and gypsies used to visit his grave. Their gatherings became so boisterous that the rector decided they must end and special constables were enrolled. But when the gypsies next returned and their queen was locked out of the church, in reprisal they smashed everything they could find.

That evening, after visiting the inn, the queen came back to the churchyard. Standing on the wall, she uttered her curse. She told the rector he would not be preaching there at that time next year. She predicted two years bad luck for the church-warden. She vowed that the sexton would be buried next year. She told two special constables, who were half-gypsy brothers, that they would "die together, sudden and quick." Finally she cursed the church door, saying that anyone who locked it would die within a year.

It all came true. The rector had a stroke and never preached again. The Church-warden's cows went sick, his crops failed and his wife's babies were still-born. The sexton died of a heart attack. The two special constables vanished, never to be seen again. (Two tall skeletons found in a shallow grave near Odstock, many years later, were thought to be theirs.)

The church door was locked twice after being

cursed. Both of the men who locked it died within a year. A later rector threw the door key into the river, which seemed to him the wisest thing to do.

The Potterne Witch

Not so long ago, a man used to walk over to Potterne after work, to see his fiancee who lived there with her mother. Whenever they went for their evening stroll, a greyhound would always follow them.

One wet evening as they walked back to the girl's house, the greyhound overtook them, jumped the garden gate and disappeared. On reaching the house and looking through the window, the man saw the mother washing mud from her legs as she stood in a shallow bath. Then it dawned on him that she had a witch's power to change herself into a greyhound.

TRADITIONAL CURES AND HERBS

Here is a very unusual old Dorset cure for toothache. Make a slit in a young oak tree: cut a bit of your hair off: put it in the slit and with your hand on the tree, say: "This I bequeath to the oak tree. In the name of the Father, and of the Son, and of the Holy Ghost. Amen."

Sore eyes could be soothed by bathing them in water taken from an east-facing spring, preferably when first lit by the sun's rays. An old, rather off-putting remedy for jaundice was to eat nine lice on a piece of bread and butter. Quinsy could be kept away by wearing a band of silk round the neck.

A Purbeck parson was once asked by a mother whether he minded if a cup was stolen from him by her daughter. She believed that fits were curable by crockery taken unawares from a clergyman, powdered and eaten.

A headache could by eased by wearing a snake skin in the hat. An effective remedy for boils was to crawl under a bramble on three consecutive mornings against the sun just as it rose. The plant comfrey had great healing powers and was used to bathe cuts and scratches.

A cure for bronchitis was to take nine hairs from the back of a white she-ass, sew them in a silk bag and wear it round the neck. A child could be cured of whooping-cough by circulating it three times over and under a donkey's body.

Ralph Whitlock has recorded a variety of old Wessex cures for warts. One way was by covering the wart with a cobweb, which was afterwards burnt. Another reliable method was to steal a piece of raw steak, rub it on the wart and bury it secretly in the ground. The wart would disappear as the steak rotted away.

Elder could be substituted for steak. A young elder shoot was cut and on it carved as many notches as there were warts to be got rid of. It was then buried and the warts vanished as the shoot decayed. But they would be transferred to anyone who found it and picked it up.

Yet another remedy was to rub the wart with the blood of small animals such as moles, mice and cats. Herbal cures of all kinds were tried, involving the juices from fig leaves, dandelion stems, the greater celandine and many other plants.

To Prevent Cramp

One way to ward off the racking pains of cramp at night was to put corks under the pillow or tie them round the limb which might be attacked. A hag stone under the bed or a magnet with points towards the foot of the bed were also effective. Moles' feet were frequently carried to prevent cramp.

Herbs feature prominently in Kathleen Wiltshire's fascinating folklore writings. Marjoram was often used in old-time cures: its oil soothed toothache and its tea kept infection from chest and lungs. It was also made into drops to relieve earache.

The nettle was another "cure-all". It was specially good for glandular troubles and gout. A daily massage with its oil prevented dandruff. Young nettle-tops, boiled with sugar, provided a splendid blood purifier.

Many herbal recipes were based on rosemary. The liquid produced by boiling its leaves in white wine was a reliable cough mixture and also a tonic for lost appetite. Infusions of rosemary were good for heart complaints and high blood pressure. The leaves, bound in linen cloth, were often applied to those parts afflicted with gout.

They called rue "the herb of grace" but it was also said that naughty nuns devoured the leaves as a contraceptive before an orgy. As rue kept joints and tendons free from deposits, it frequently appeared in the treatment of arthritis, sciatica and lumbago. Rue was considered doubly potent if stolen from someone else's garden.

WHAT'S IN A NAME?

Dorset countryfolk had some very expressive names for their birds and beasts. A donkey was a "nirrup" and a pig was a "mallock". Field-mice were called "mouels" and the shrew-mouse was a "shrowcrop". A scolding woman must have got the name of shrew from its shrill shrieking. A cuckoo was a "gawky" and a duck was a "homble".

The robin's red breast would account for it being called a "ruddock", while the green wood-pecker's name of "yaffle" came from its discordant cry. A wren was a "cut" and a wood-pigeon was a "culver".

The word "mommet" had several different meanings. Around Shaftesbury, someone who caused annoyance would be called "a silly mommet". In another part of North Dorset, it was used for any animal that was stubborn or went the wrong way.

Elsewhere it meant a scarecrow or a bogeyman or a witch's wax doll. The parson — poet William Barnes, who was very clue-ed up on Dorset dialect, defined it as a guy or an effigy.

Ralph Whitlock, a farmer's son, has recalled some of the words once commonly used in Wiltshire fields and cottages. Sheaves stood to dry in "hiles" and hay was gathered in "pooks". Garden plots were measured in "lugs", which equalled a rod, pole or perch. Ricks and cottage roofs were thatched with "yealms" or "elums", which were bundles of straw thatching.

A loft was a "tallet" and a granary was a "gurner". "Bavvins" were the brushwood faggots burnt in lime-kilns and bread-ovens. A sieve was a "rudder". The mushroom-like stones which under-propped ricks and granaries to exclude the rats were "staddles".

hands in a small barrel called a "plough-bottle". A "kivver" contained bread. A morning snack or lunch, taken at 9 o'clock, was known as "nammit". In the afternoon, a 3 o'clock snack was a "jewbit". "Nammit" was used too for the first slice from a loaf, which had the alternative name of "kissy bread".

SOME DORSET SAYINGS

As you might expect, Thomas Hardy's works include many of the old Wessex proverbial sayings. Here is one out of "Far from the Madding Crowd": "Better wed over the mixen than over the moor." This implied that it was safer to marry someone from your own part than a stanger from further away.

Another saying from "A Changed Man" advised against trying to do too much and went: "Better a little fire to warm 'ee than a great one to burn 'ee." "One onion is enough for a whole parish," summed up the powerful effects of that vegetable.

"If you sing before breakfast, you'll cry before night," warned that there was more in life than laughter. Anything that happened quickly was said to have been done "in the twinkling of a cock-sparrow's eyebrow."

Shaftesbury was the subject of an insulting old maxim which claimed that it had "more beer than water: more rogues than honest folk: and the churchyard higher than the church."

The Flying Monk

WILTSHIRE'S CURIOUS CHARACTERS

The Flying Monk

The historian William of Malmesbury recorded the story of Brother Oliver, a Saxon monk and pioneer aviator:-

> "He was a man of good learning for those times, of mature age and in his early youth had hazarded an attempt of singular temerity. He had by some contrivance fastened wings to his hands and feet, in order that, looking upon the fable as true, he might fly like Daedalus, and collecting the air on the summit of a tower, had flown for more than the distance of a furlong; but, agitated by the violence of the wind and the current of air, he fell and broke both his legs, and was lame ever after. He used to relate as the cause of his failure, his forgetting to provide himself with a tail."

The tower mentioned was that of Malmesbury Abbey.

Rattlebone

The heroic John Rattlebone took part in a great battle at Sherston between Saxons and Danes in 1016. Neither side won but during the fighting he was horribly wounded in the stomach. His guts began to gush out but, grabbing a tile, he held it to his wound and fought on to the end.

He must have survived because he was awarded the manor of Sherston for his bravery. He is remembered in an old song:

"Fight well Rattlebone
Thou shalt have Sherstone."
"What will I with Sherstone do
Save with all that belongs thereto?"
"Thou shalt have Wych and Wellesley,
Easton Town and Pinkeney."

The village inn is called the Rattlebone and its sign shows him holding his tile. In the church a huge timber chest, with the initials "R.B." carved on it, is supposed to have held his armour.

Bonham's Babies

Sir Thomas Bonham, who lived at Great Wishford in the 15th century, fell upon hard times. So when his wife gave birth to twins, he bade her farewell and went off on a Crusade.

Nobody in Wishford recognised him when he returned seven years later. Dressed as a pilgrim, he had not shaved since leaving home. On producing an identifying ring, his wife welcomed him back and the following year seven babies were born to her all at the same time.

They were taken in a sieve for baptism in the church, where it was later hung up. In 1828, three old villagers could remember seeing it there when young.

Tradition has it that a local witch brought Sir Thomas back, just as his wife was about to marry again, having given him up for lost.

Maud Heath

The widow Maud Heath has no less than three memorials to her credit. Five centuries ago, she used to tramp through the marshes from her home at Langley Burrell with butter and eggs for Chippenham Market. She must have made a fair living because she left enough money to provide a proper path, so that future generations could travel dry shod.

The result, still visible and 4½ miles long, is known as Maud Heath's Causeway. It starts at Wick Hill, where her statue looks down from the top of a column. In bonnet and homespun dress, she sits holding a stick and a basket.

At Kellaways, where the causeway runs over sixty-four arches, she has a sun-dial inscribed: "Injure me not" and in Chippenham, by Saint Paul's church, stands an upright stone also suitably inscribed.

Ruth Pierce

In Devizes Market Place, an impressive monument records this curious incident:

> "On Thursday, the 25th of January, 1753, Ruth Pierce, of Potterne, in this County, agreed with three other women to buy a sack of wheat in the Market, each paying her due proportion towards the same. One of these women, in collecting the several quotas of money, discovered a deficiency, and demanded of Ruth Pierce the sum which was wanted to make good the amount. Ruth Pierce protested she had paid her share and said "She wished she

might drop down dead if she had not." She rashly repeated this awful wish, when, to the consternation and terror of the surrounding multitude, she instantly fell down and expired having the money concealed in her hand."
The amount involved was threepence.

The Wiltshire Moonrakers

The most famous of all the county's folk-tales concerns the Wiltshire Moonrakers. The story goes that some smugglers of Bishops Cannings had hidden a number of brandy kegs in the village pond. One night while trying to retrieve them with the aid of wooden hayrakes, they were surprised by a patrol of Excisemen.

Asked what they were doing, the smugglers, with a flash of inspiration, pretended to be nut-cases. Pointing to the reflection of the full moon on the water, they replied: "We be a-reaking for thik thur girt cheese." The patrol rode off, laughing at such stupidity.

But the smugglers kept their brandy and to this day Wiltshiremen are still known as Moonrakers.

Perhaps the story of the Moonrakers puts the lighter side of Wessex folklore in a nutshell. But Thomas Hardy sums up the other side — charms, witchcraft and folk-medecine — in that single tremendous oath from "The Mayor of Casterbridge":

"By the sun, moon, and stars,
by the clouds, the winds, the trees;
likewise by the cats' eyes, the ravens,
the leeches, the spiders, and the dung-mixen,
the last fortnight in August
will be rain and tempest."